The Usborne
HUMAN BODY
Sticker Book

Alex Frith

Illustrated by Ian McNee and Adam Larkum

Designed by Stephen Moncrieff and Emily Barden

Human body expert: Dr. Zoë Fritz

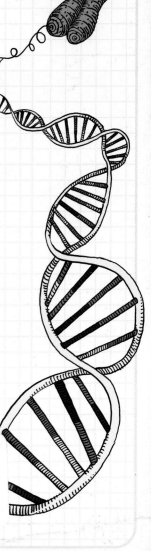

Contents

D0319398

WHAT ARE BODIES MADE OF?

The human body is made up of different types of body tissue, including bone, muscle and organs, which are built up in layers. Tiny networks, or systems, of tubes connect together the different layers.

MUSCLES

Directly beneath the skin is a layer of fat, and beneath that is layer of muscle.

BONES

Beneath most muscles are bones. They join together to form the skeleton.

GRAVE SECRETS

In order to find out how bodies work, doctors often cut open dead people. This is called *dissection*. For long periods of history, it was illegal – doctors had to pay grave diggers to find them fresh bodies.

VITAL ORGANS

Beneath some parts of the skeleton are many soft body parts, known as organs, that work together to keep the body alive.

People can survive without some organs, such as the eyes, but others, such as the liver and brain, are vital for life.

HUMAN ANATOMY

Soon after dissection became legal, young British doctors Henry Gray and Henry Carter spent two years dissecting bodies and drawing pictures of what they found. In 1858 they published a book, called *Gray's Anatomy*, which is still used to teach doctors today.

CIRCULATORY SYSTEM

Blood travels around the body through a long series of tubes, circulating oxygen to every organ and muscle.

NERVOUS SYSTEM

A network of nerves sends signals between the brain and every part of the body.

LYMPHATIC SYSTEM

A system of tubes runs between most organs. The tubes contains a liquid called *lymph*, which helps keep the body healthy.

Lymph gathers in lumps called lymph nodes, shown as green dots.

HOW DO BODIES WORK?

To make sure each organ is doing the right thing at the right time, the body sends chemical messages, known as *hormones*, through the blood. Hormones are made in small organs called *glands*.

● THYROID GLAND
Releases *thyroxine*, a hormone that speeds up and slows down how fast the body works.

● PANCREAS
Releases *insulin* and *glucagon*, hormones that control the amount of sugar in the blood.

● ADRENAL GLANDS
Release *adrenaline*, a hormone that makes a person alert and active when danger is near.

● PINEAL GLAND
Releases *melatonin*, a hormone to tell the body to sleep.

● PITUITARY GLAND
Releases hormones that tells other glands when it's time to release their hormones.

Major glands

Use the stickers to add glands to this body.

HORMONE HISTORY

The first hormone was discovered in 1902 by William Bayliss and Ernest Starling. They were studying how the body knew when to start digesting food.

Skeleton and Bones

An adult skeleton is made up of around 206 bones. Children have more, but some of them fuse together as they grow up. Bones and teeth are so tough, they can stay intact for hundreds of years after death.

Inside a Bone

Bones have a tough outer layer and a soft inner layer. Many bones contain a central layer of something called bone marrow, too.

Compact bone

Bone marrow, where blood is made

Spongy bone

Cross section through a thigh bone

2nd-century Greek physician Galen wanted to map out the skeleton, but didn't dare dissect a human body. Instead, he made drawings based on ape skeletons.

For centuries, doctors in Europe learned anatomy by studying Galen's work.

In the 16th century, Flemish physician Andreas Vesalius was one of the first people to examine human skeletons. He uncovered errors in Galen's work, and corrected them.

Use the stickers to complete this skeleton.

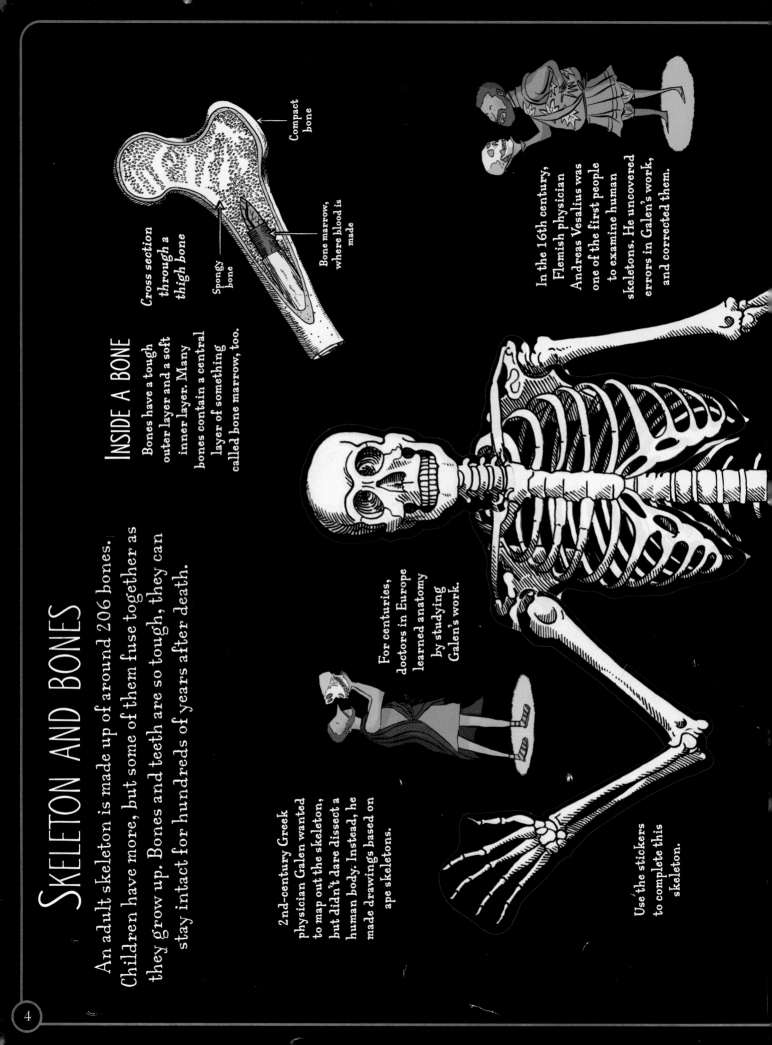

Each hand is made of 27 bones:
Five *metacarpals* connect the wrist to the fingers and thumb.

Each finger is made of three *phalanges*. The thumb is made of two.

Eight *carpals* in the wrist

X-RAYS

Doctors use a device called an X-ray machine to see a person's bones inside their body. The power of X-rays to shine through skin was discovered by German scientist Wilhelm Röntgen in 1896.

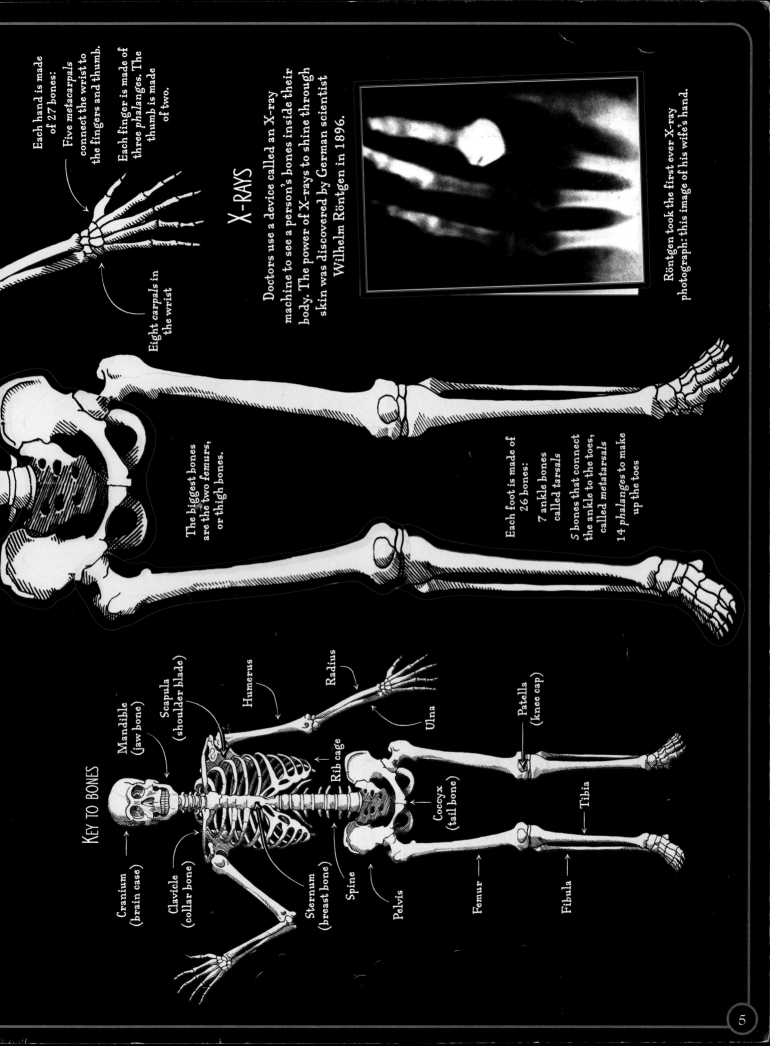

Röntgen took the first ever X-ray photograph: this image of his wife's hand.

The biggest bones are the two *femurs*, or thigh bones.

Each foot is made of 26 bones:
7 ankle bones called *tarsals*
5 bones that connect the ankle to the toes, called *metatarsals*
14 *phalanges* to make up the toes

KEY TO BONES

Cranium (brain case)

Mandible (jaw bone)

Clavicle (collar bone)

Scapula (shoulder blade)

Humerus

Radius

Rib cage

Ulna

Sternum (breast bone)

Spine

Coccyx (tail bone)

Patella (knee cap)

Pelvis

Femur

Tibia

Fibula

MUSCLE POWER

There are around 640 muscles working in pairs or small groups to make the body move. They are known as *skeletal muscles*.

MUSCLE PAIRS

Muscles that bend joints are called *flexors*. Muscles that straighten joints are called *extensors*.

Deltoid moves the shoulder.

Pectoralis Major moves the chest.

Biceps bends the elbow.

External Oblique moves the side.

Abdominals bend the body.

Gluteus Medius swivels the hip.

Sartorius lifts the leg and flexes the knee. It is the longest muscle in the body.

Trapezius keeps the shoulder straight.

Deltoid

Triceps straightens the arm.

Latissimus twists the back.

Gluteus maximus

Three muscles known as hamstrings help you walk, run and jump.

Use the stickers to complete this muscle figure.

MUSCLE TISSUE

Skeletal muscle is made in layers. Dark layers burn energy more than the white layers, but they tire out more quickly.

This photograph shows a section of skeletal muscle in the lip, magnified to 64 times life size.

MUSCLES AND BRAINS

In the 17th century, Dutch biologist Jan Swammerdam killed a frog and poked its brain with a stick. Even though it was dead, its legs twitched. This showed that the brain, rather than any other organ, makes muscles move.

MUSCLES AND BONES

Muscles are connected to bones by parts called *tendons*. When a muscle contracts, it pulls on the tendon, making the bone move.

Bones are connected to each other by parts called *ligaments*.

Tendon

Muscle

Muscles and bones in a human hand

BICEPS AND TRICEPS

Two muscles in the upper arms, called the *biceps* and the *triceps*, work as a pair to make each arm bend.

Flexor muscle

Biceps

When the biceps contracts, the arm bends.

Extensor muscle

When the triceps contracts, the arm straightens.

Triceps

Cross section of skeletal muscle

Skeletal muscles are made up of bundles of long tubes called *myocytes*. These contain even tinier tubes called *myofibrils*.

Bone

Tendon

Myocyte

Myofibril

BIOELECTRICITY

For a long time, doctors thought muscles inflated with air or some kind of fluid to flex. In 1791, Italian scientist Luigi Galvani used a dead frog to prove them wrong. He connected the legs of the frog to an electric current, and watched them twitch.

Because there was no fluid inside the dead frog, Galvani realized the muscles must be activated by electricity instead. Scientists now describe the signals that nerves send as *bioelectricity*.

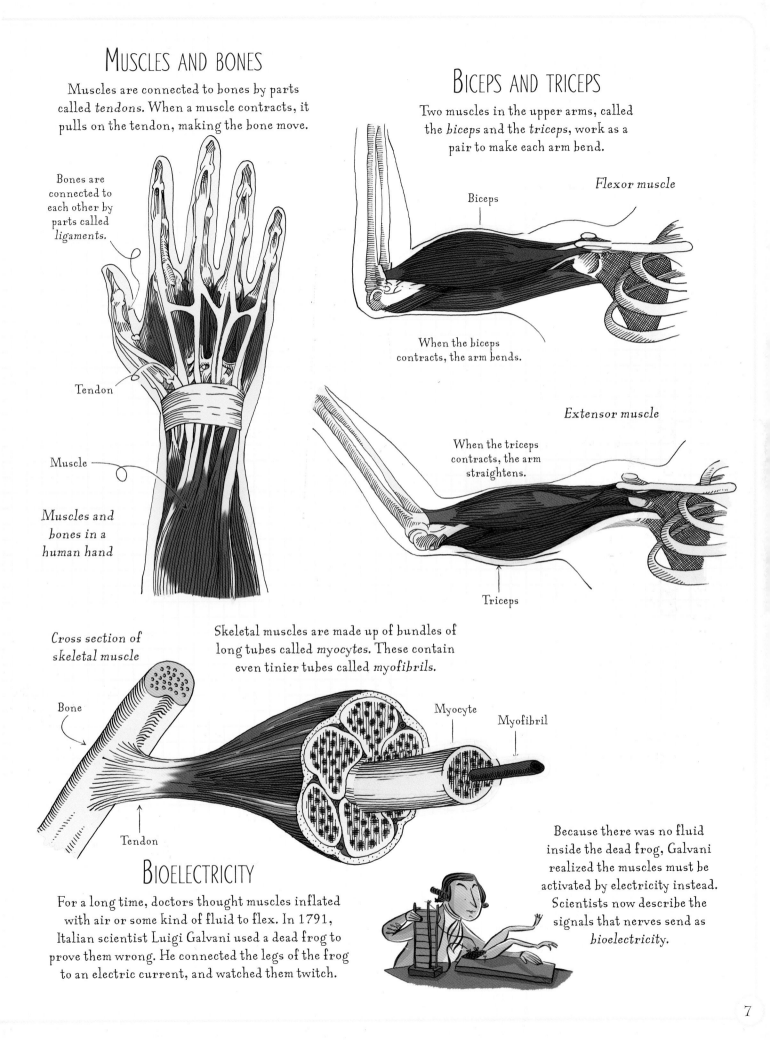

CIRCULATION

With every breath, the lungs take in oxygen from the air and pass it into the bloodstream. The heart pumps blood, and the oxygen in it, all over the body. This is called *circulation*.

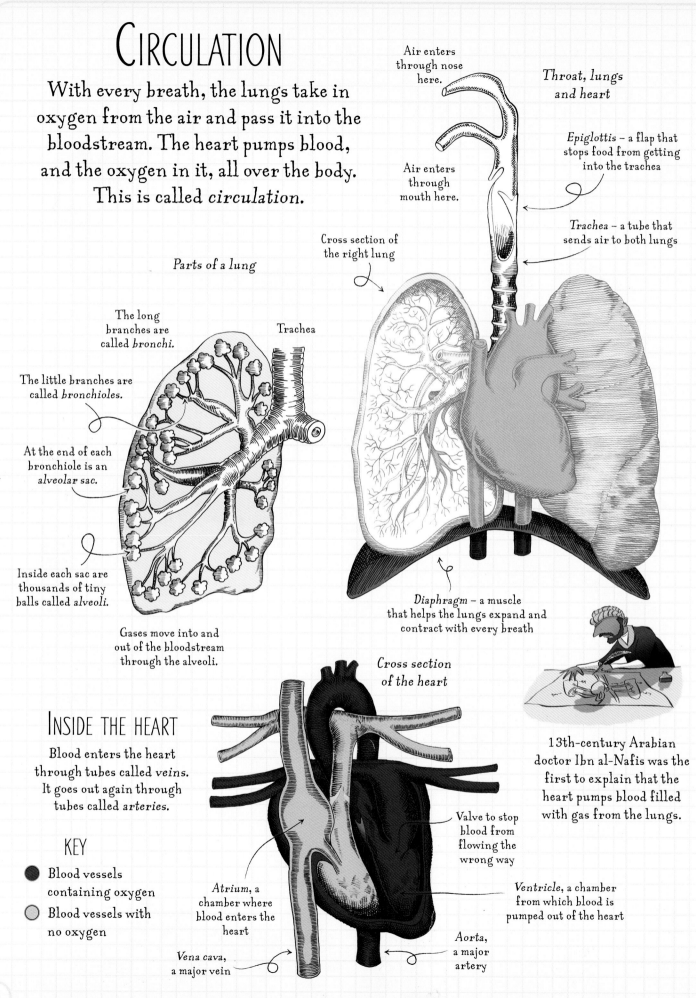

Air enters through nose here.

Air enters through mouth here.

Throat, lungs and heart

Epiglottis – a flap that stops food from getting into the trachea

Trachea – a tube that sends air to both lungs

Cross section of the right lung

Parts of a lung

The long branches are called *bronchi*.

Trachea

The little branches are called *bronchioles*.

At the end of each bronchiole is an *alveolar sac*.

Inside each sac are thousands of tiny balls called *alveoli*.

Gases move into and out of the bloodstream through the alveoli.

Diaphragm – a muscle that helps the lungs expand and contract with every breath

Cross section of the heart

INSIDE THE HEART

Blood enters the heart through tubes called *veins*. It goes out again through tubes called *arteries*.

KEY

● Blood vessels containing oxygen

○ Blood vessels with no oxygen

Atrium, a chamber where blood enters the heart

Vena cava, a major vein

Valve to stop blood from flowing the wrong way

Ventricle, a chamber from which blood is pumped out of the heart

Aorta, a major artery

13th-century Arabian doctor Ibn al-Nafis was the first to explain that the heart pumps blood filled with gas from the lungs.

8

CIRCULATION IN ACTION

Follow the diagram to see what happens in the bloodstream between breaths.

① Air containing oxygen enters the lungs.

17th-century British physician William Harvey was the first doctor to describe circulation. He discovered the process through treating badly wounded soldiers.

② Oxygen passes into the alveoli, and then into the bloodstream. It travels straight to the heart through the *pulmonary vein*.

⑦ Carbon dioxide passes from the bloodstream back into the alveoli, and is breathed out.

Alveoli

Alveoli

Upper vena cava

Upper aorta

Pulmonary vein

⑥ The heart relaxes, and blood with carbon dioxide in returns along the vena cava back into the heart.

③ The heart contracts, squeezing oxygenated blood into the aorta, sending oxygen all over the body.

Lower aorta

⑤ When organs and muscles do anything, they use up oxygen and produce a waste gas called carbon dioxide. Carbon dioxide passes into veins.

Lower vena cava

Diaphragm

④ A network of smaller arteries carries blood from the aorta to organs such as the liver, and muscles such as the diaphragm. Here, the oxygen is combined with energy from food to do work.

Liver

KEY

→ Route taken by oxygen

→ Route taken by carbon dioxide

● Blood containing oxygen

○ Blood with no oxygen

Oxygen is carried inside tiny balls known as *red blood cells*. It takes around 20 seconds for each cell to travel along the whole circulatory system.

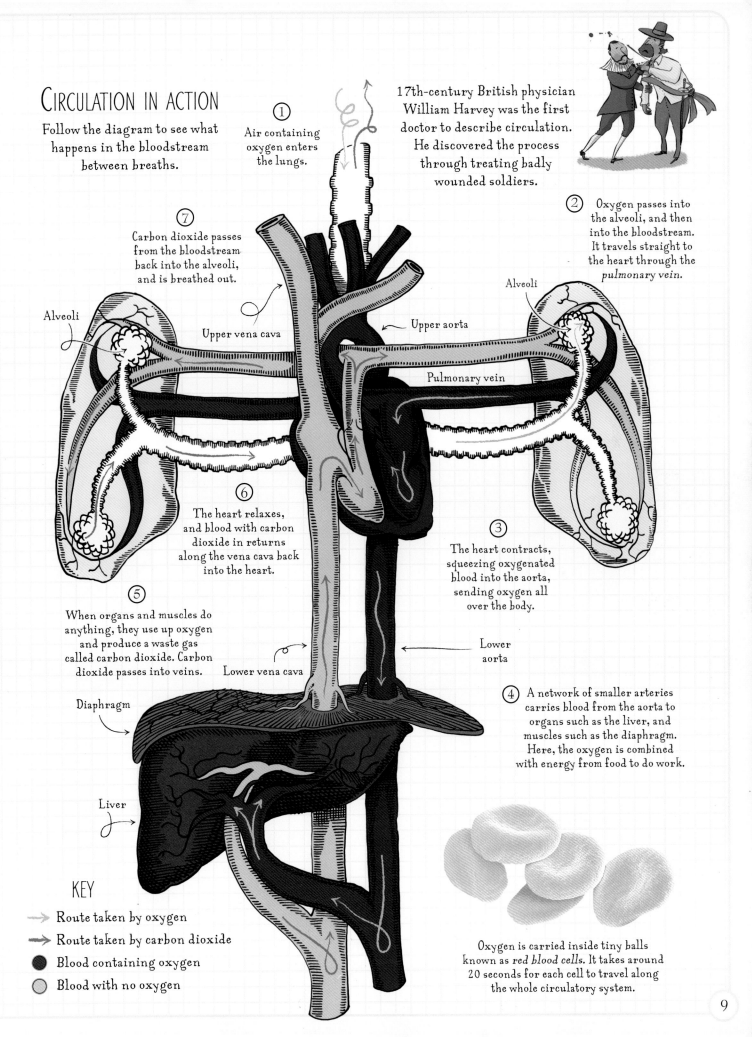

PROCESSING FOOD

To get energy and to keep healthy, the body needs nutrients from food and drink. A system of organs, called the *digestive system*, breaks food down and extracts those nutrients, a process that takes around three days.

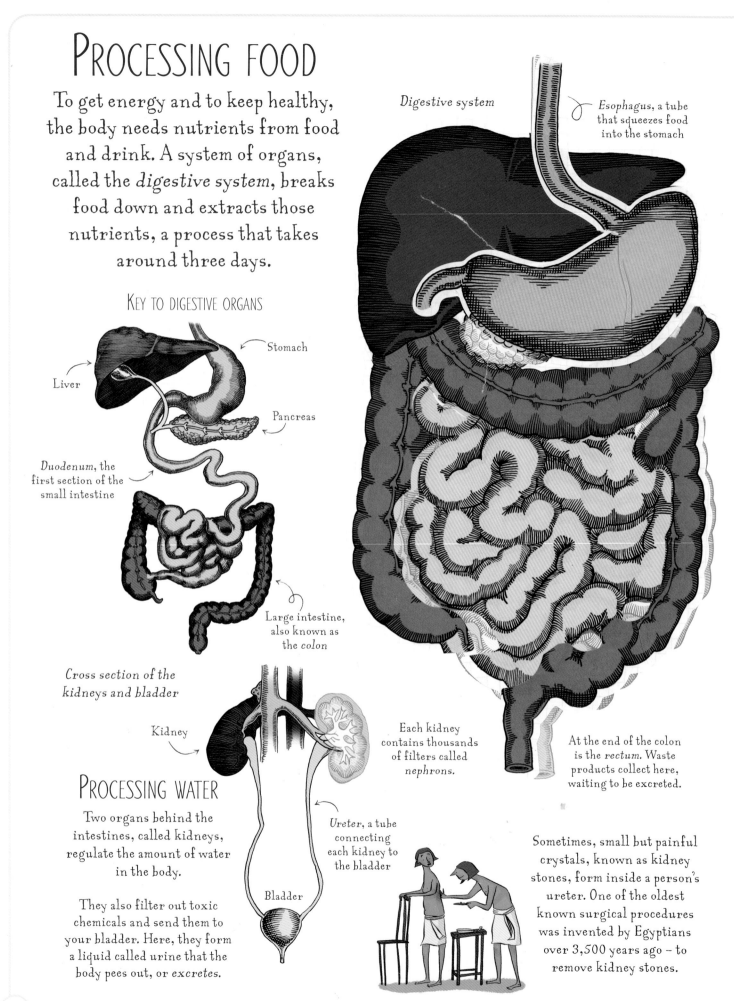

Digestive system

Esophagus, a tube that squeezes food into the stomach

KEY TO DIGESTIVE ORGANS

Stomach

Liver

Pancreas

Duodenum, the first section of the small intestine

Large intestine, also known as the *colon*

Cross section of the kidneys and bladder

Kidney

Each kidney contains thousands of filters called *nephrons*.

At the end of the colon is the *rectum*. Waste products collect here, waiting to be excreted.

PROCESSING WATER

Two organs behind the intestines, called kidneys, regulate the amount of water in the body.

Ureter, a tube connecting each kidney to the bladder

Bladder

They also filter out toxic chemicals and send them to your bladder. Here, they form a liquid called urine that the body pees out, or *excretes*.

Sometimes, small but painful crystals, known as kidney stones, form inside a person's ureter. One of the oldest known surgical procedures was invented by Egyptians over 3,500 years ago – to remove kidney stones.

WHERE FOOD GOES

Use the stickers to reveal cutaway diagrams of the major organs involved in digestion. Find out what happens to food as it passes along the digestive system.

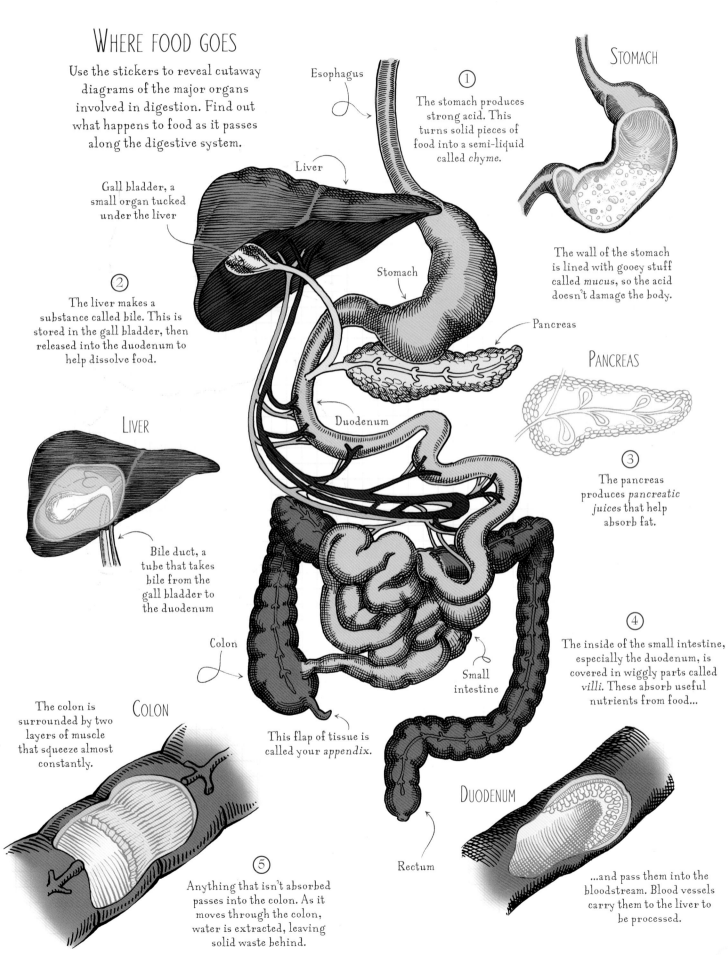

Esophagus

Liver

Gall bladder, a small organ tucked under the liver

Stomach

Pancreas

Duodenum

STOMACH

① The stomach produces strong acid. This turns solid pieces of food into a semi-liquid called *chyme*.

The wall of the stomach is lined with gooey stuff called *mucus*, so the acid doesn't damage the body.

PANCREAS

③ The pancreas produces *pancreatic juices* that help absorb fat.

② The liver makes a substance called bile. This is stored in the gall bladder, then released into the duodenum to help dissolve food.

LIVER

Bile duct, a tube that takes bile from the gall bladder to the duodenum

Colon

Small intestine

This flap of tissue is called your *appendix*.

④ The inside of the small intestine, especially the duodenum, is covered in wiggly parts called *villi*. These absorb useful nutrients from food...

The colon is surrounded by two layers of muscle that squeeze almost constantly.

COLON

DUODENUM

Rectum

⑤ Anything that isn't absorbed passes into the colon. As it moves through the colon, water is extracted, leaving solid waste behind.

...and pass them into the bloodstream. Blood vessels carry them to the liver to be processed.

Brain power

The brain controls many of the body's functions, and allows a person to choose what to do with their body, too.

The *cerebral cortex* is the outermost part of the brain. It controls thinking and memory.

Left and right

The brain has left and right halves. If one half stops working, the other can keep a person going.

Cross section of the brain

The *corpus callosum* is a bridge that connects the two halves of the brain.

Eyeball

Pituitary gland, a gland that activates many hormones

The *hypothalamus* connects the nervous system to the hormone system.

The *pons* connects the brainstem to the brain.

The *brainstem* connects the brain to the rest of the nervous system.

The *cerebellum* controls movement.

The *medulla oblongata* automatically controls circulation and other vital operations.

Lumps and bumps

In the 19th century, some doctors believed they could trace the shape of a person's brain by feeling lumps on their head, an idea known as *phrenology*.

Phrenologists made charts connecting parts of the brain to different mental skills and personality traits.

This is a phrenology chart, drawn in the 1920s. Phrenologists used these charts to decide what a person was good at by feeling lumps on their heads. Scientists now know this doesn't work.

Looking into the brain

Today, scientists can look directly at a living brain. They use scanners to see where blood is flowing fastest when a person carries out tasks. This helps them build up a map of how the brain works.

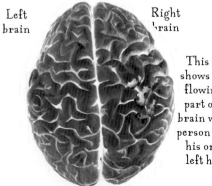

Left brain

Right brain

This scan shows blood flowing to part of the brain when a person moves his or her left hand.

BUILD A BRAIN

Scientists find it helpful to divide the brain into sections called *lobes*. Use the lobe stickers to build up a whole brain.

- Frontal lobe, which helps with decison making
- Parietal lobe, which helps you identify and pick up objects
- Temporal lobe, which stores long term memories
- Occipital lobe, which processes vision
- Brainstem, which helps control a body's sleep cycle

Each lobe carries out many different tasks. They can even take on extra tasks if other lobes are damaged.

Brains have two temporal lobes – one on each side.

People can survive even if parts of their frontal lobe are damaged or removed.

The frontal, parietal and occipital lobes are all split into two halves, joined by the corpus callosum.

BRAIN MAP

Different parts of the brain control different parts of the mind and body. Here are a few examples:

Thinking about other people

Movement   Touch

Processing information about the self

Some areas of the brain are still a mystery to scientists.

Helps combine information from all the senses

Vision

Processing likes and dislikes

Smell

Processing emotions

Balance and coordination

Breathing and circulation

Connections across the whole brain store all kinds of memories.

NEURONS

The brain is made of billions of cells called *neurons*. They are linked in a gigantic network.

A neuron

Tiny branches called *dendrites* connect each neuron to many other neurons.

The head of the neuron is called the *soma*.

A thick strand, called the axon, conducts electrical signals away from the soma.

HOLE IN THE HEAD

A major breakthrough in brain science happened after an accident in the USA in 1848. Railway worker Phineas Gage was hit by an iron bar, which made a hole in his frontal lobe.

He survived, but his personality changed. Doctors who studied him concluded that the frontal lobe helps to control a person's temper.

Sensing the world

Brains use five senses – sight, sound, smell, touch and taste – to perceive the world. The process begins in the brain, which comes up with a rough picture of what it expects to perceive. Nerve signals from the five senses fill in the details.

A network of nerves connects sense receptors to the brain.

How eyes see

Light travels through each eyeball and onto a light sensitive part of the eye called the *retina*. Nerves in the retina send signals to the brain.

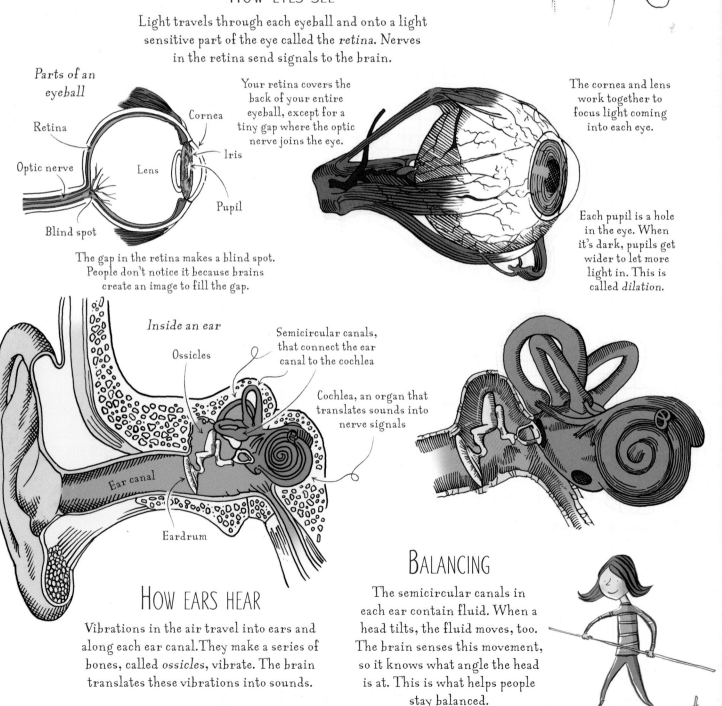

Parts of an eyeball

Retina

Cornea

Optic nerve

Lens

Iris

Pupil

Blind spot

Your retina covers the back of your entire eyeball, except for a tiny gap where the optic nerve joins the eye.

The gap in the retina makes a blind spot. People don't notice it because brains create an image to fill the gap.

The cornea and lens work together to focus light coming into each eye.

Each pupil is a hole in the eye. When it's dark, pupils get wider to let more light in. This is called *dilation*.

Inside an ear

Ossicles

Semicircular canals, that connect the ear canal to the cochlea

Cochlea, an organ that translates sounds into nerve signals

Ear canal

Eardrum

How ears hear

Vibrations in the air travel into ears and along each ear canal. They make a series of bones, called *ossicles*, vibrate. The brain translates these vibrations into sounds.

Balancing

The semicircular canals in each ear contain fluid. When a head tilts, the fluid moves, too. The brain senses this movement, so it knows what angle the head is at. This is what helps people stay balanced.

HOW NOSES SMELL

Nerves at the top of the nasal cavity pick up smells from tiny particles that get in through the nostrils and the mouth.

HOW TONGUES TASTE

Taste buds, found all over the top of the tongue, can distinguish between at least four different types of tastes: sweet, sour, salty and bitter.

Most of the tongue is covered in tiny bumps called *papillae*. Some contain taste buds; others help break up food so it can be digested. This photo shows papillae at 165 times actual size.

SENSING YOURSELF

The link between your nerves and brain lets you know what position your body is in. That's how you can tell where your hands are, even when you can't see them.

This sense is called *proprioception*.

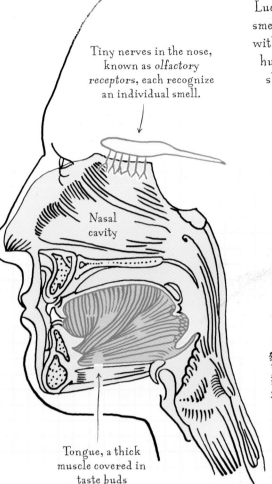

Tiny nerves in the nose, known as *olfactory receptors*, each recognize an individual smell.

Nasal cavity

Tongue, a thick muscle covered in taste buds

WHAT IS SMELL?

Ancient Roman philosopher Lucretius suggested that every smell is caused by tiny particles with a different shape, and that human brains match up these shapes to particular smells.

In 2004, two American biologists proved that Lucretius was correct.

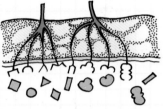

Olfactory receptors each detect a specific smell particle.

HOW SKIN FEELS

Skin contains four types of nerve endings, called *receptors*, that pick up different sensations.

Close up of nerve endings in skin

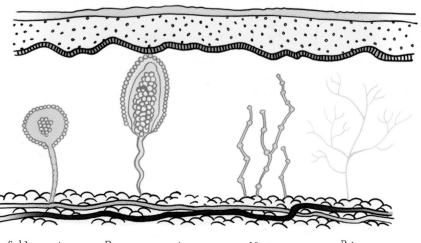

Cold receptor   Pressure receptor   Heat receptor   Pain receptor

LOOKING CLOSER

All body tissue is made of billions and billions of tiny building blocks called cells. Different organs and tissues are made of different types of cells. Most are so tiny they can only be seen under a microscope.

UP CLOSE

Normal laboratory microscopes are powerful enough to show cells in great detail. Computerized equipment such as electron microscopes can show even greater detail, including the molecules cells are made of.

These three individual cheek cells are shown at 1,000 times their actual size.

This is a cluster of cells from the inside of a person's cheek, magnified to 100 times actual size.

Cells are made up of many parts, known as *organelles*, seen here as little specks inside the cells.

Cells were first discovered and named by British scientist Robert Hooke in 1665. He found them when he was looking at plants through a powerful microscope.

LIVING IN YOUR SKIN

17th-century Dutch lens grinder Antonie van Leeuwenhoek built one of the first really powerful microscopes. He discovered human body cells, and something else as well...

Van Leeuwenhoek's microscope

Spike to hold specimens

Lens

Van Leeuwenhoek's assistant, Anna Lister, drew these pictures of animalcules.

...hundreds and hundreds of tiny creatures living on and in human bodies. He called these creatures *animalcules*. Scientists today call them *micro-organisms*.

Most micro-organisms are harmless, but some can cause diseases. Find out more on page 22.

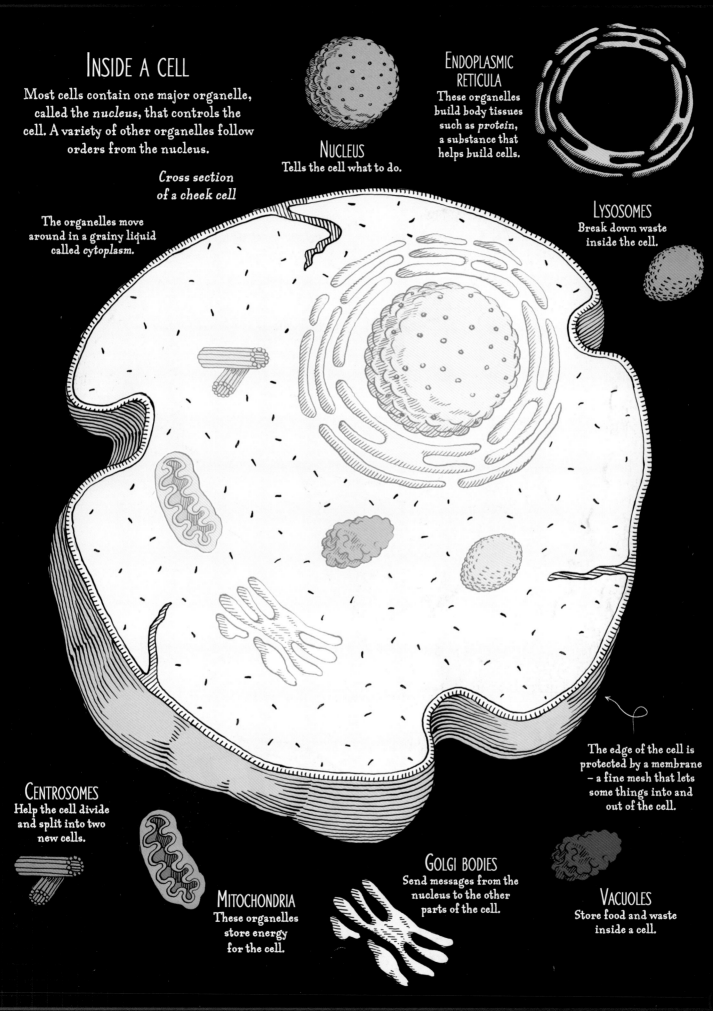

INSIDE A CELL

Most cells contain one major organelle, called the *nucleus*, that controls the cell. A variety of other organelles follow orders from the nucleus.

Cross section of a cheek cell

The organelles move around in a grainy liquid called *cytoplasm*.

NUCLEUS
Tells the cell what to do.

ENDOPLASMIC RETICULA
These organelles build body tissues such as *protein*, a substance that helps build cells.

LYSOSOMES
Break down waste inside the cell.

The edge of the cell is protected by a membrane – a fine mesh that lets some things into and out of the cell.

CENTROSOMES
Help the cell divide and split into two new cells.

MITOCHONDRIA
These organelles store energy for the cell.

GOLGI BODIES
Send messages from the nucleus to the other parts of the cell.

VACUOLES
Store food and waste inside a cell.

THE SECRET IN THE CELLS

All cells, except red blood cells, are controlled by a
nucleus – but how does each nucleus know what to
do? The secret is found in a long chain of chemicals
known as deoxyribonucleic acid, or *DNA*.

Cutaway of a cell

CHROMOSOMES

Inside each nucleus, DNA is
divided into 46 different blobs
called *chromosomes*.

Each chromosome is an
incredibly dense coil of DNA.

This photo shows human chromosomes
magnified to 1850 times actual
size. Like many parts of the body,
chromosomes come in pairs.

DNA DISCOVERY

The structure of DNA was
uncovered by three scientists
in the 1950s. Francis Crick
and James Watson studied
X-ray images taken by Rosalind
Franklin. Then, they built an
enormous model showing how the
chemicals in DNA join together.

GENES

In each chromosome, there are short
sections of DNA known as genes.
Genes give instructions to each cell
nucleus to do different things.

This picture shows
how a section of
DNA would look if
it was unwound.

At least 99% of genes are shared
by all people. But a 1% variation is
enough to make everyone unique.

DNA AND FAMILY

Everyone inherits DNA from their parents. That's why children often end up looking like their parents and their brothers and sisters.

Some genes are common within one family, but are not shared by everyone else. For example, this family shares a gene that makes long noses.

GENE SUPERIORITY

Everyone inherits one chromosome from each parent. Most of the genes in each chromosome are identical, but some aren't. For example, your mother might give you a gene making your eyes light, and your father for making them dark.

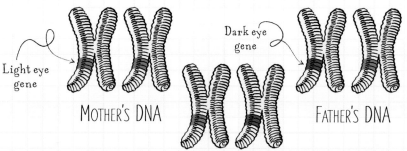

Light eye gene

Dark eye gene

MOTHER'S DNA

FATHER'S DNA

CHILD'S DNA

The 'dark eye' gene is stronger than the 'light eye' gene. This means the child, who has one of each gene, will have dark eyes.

FAMILY GENE TREE

Sometimes a child from a family of brown-eyed people can end up with blue eyes. It all depends on the pairs of genes found in their parents and grandparents. This family tree shows how.

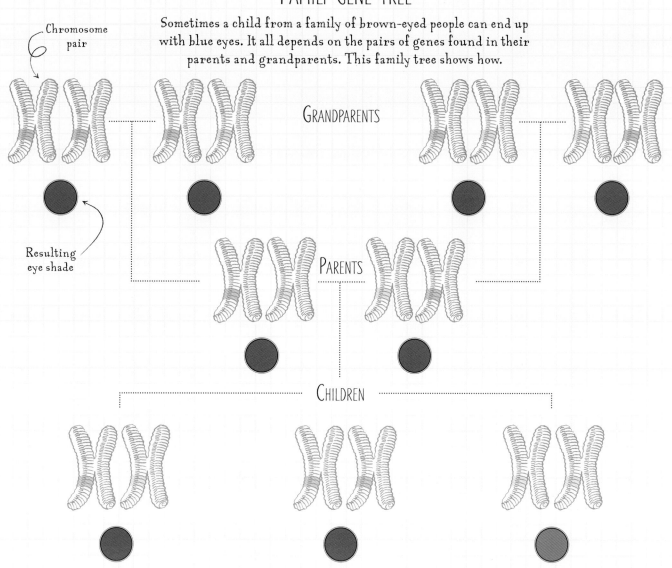

Chromosome pair

Resulting eye shade

GRANDPARENTS

PARENTS

CHILDREN

MAKING NEW BODIES

Human bodies can work in pairs to create new life. Men and women each produce cells called *gametes*. When a gamete from a man and a woman fuse together, they form the first cell of a new body.

MAKING GAMETES

Women's gametes, called *eggs*, are made by two organs called *ovaries*. The eggs come out into the *fallopian tubes*, before moving into the *uterus*.

Men's gametes, called *sperm*, are made by organs called *testes*. These hang outside the body, so the sperm don't get too hot. Sperm comes out of a man through his penis.

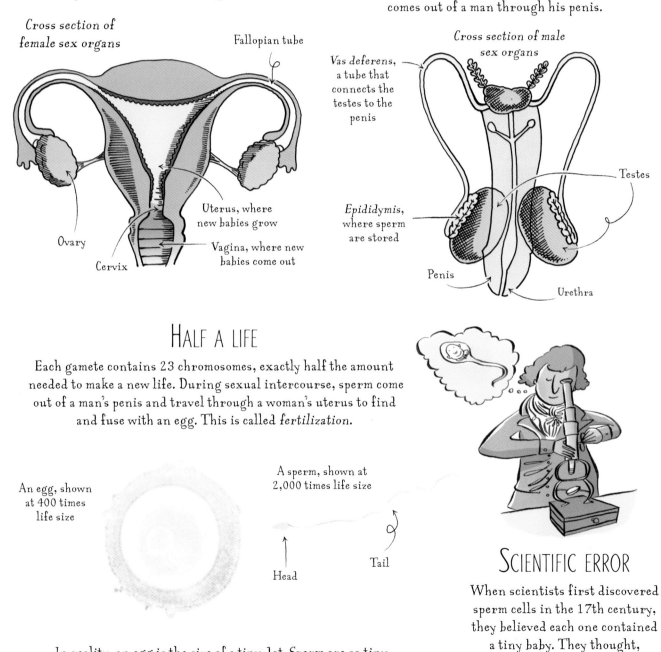

Cross section of
female sex organs

Fallopian tube

Uterus, where
new babies grow

Ovary

Cervix

Vagina, where new
babies come out

Cross section of male
sex organs

Vas deferens,
a tube that
connects the
testes to the
penis

Epididymis,
where sperm
are stored

Testes

Penis

Urethra

HALF A LIFE

Each gamete contains 23 chromosomes, exactly half the amount needed to make a new life. During sexual intercourse, sperm come out of a man's penis and travel through a woman's uterus to find and fuse with an egg. This is called *fertilization*.

An egg, shown
at 400 times
life size

A sperm, shown at
2,000 times life size

Head

Tail

In reality, an egg is the size of a tiny dot. Sperm are so tiny that thousands of them could fit inside an egg. But it only takes one sperm to fertilize an egg.

SCIENTIFIC ERROR

When scientists first discovered sperm cells in the 17th century, they believed each one contained a tiny baby. They thought, wrongly, that eggs were merely a home for that baby to grow in.

How new life grows

FERTILIZATION
The sperm fuses with the egg in the fallopian tube. The DNA mixes together, and the cell now has a full 46 chromosomes.

DAY 1: ZYGOTE
The fertilized egg divides into two cells, the first sign of new life, called a *zygote*.

DAY 3: BLASTOCYST
The cells multiply, and separate clusters of cells begin to appear, making a *blastocyst*. An outer cluster attaches to the wall of the uterus.

DAY 5: EMBRYO
There are now thousands of cells, making an *embryo*. Cells in the middle start to form a spinal cord.

WEEK 9: FETUS
By now there are too many cells to count. Some begin to form individual organs, making a *fetus*.

WEEK 40: BABY
After around nine months, the fetus has developed into a baby and is ready to be born.

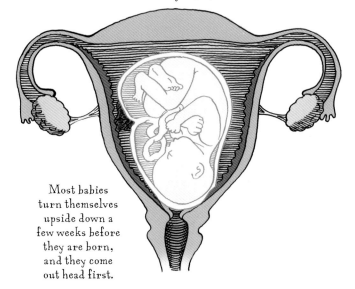

Most babies turn themselves upside down a few weeks before they are born, and they come out head first.

How a fertlized egg travels through a uterus

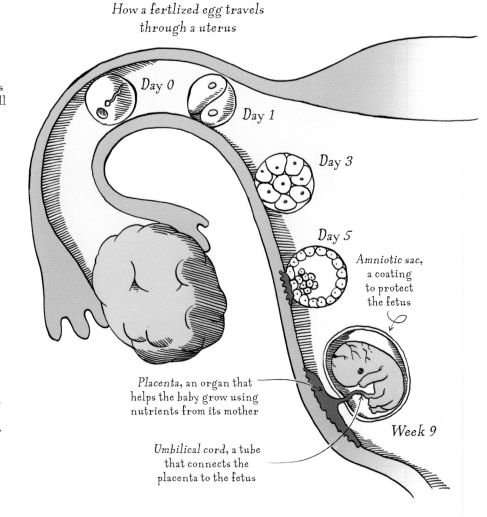

Day 0

Day 1

Day 3

Day 5

Amniotic sac, a coating to protect the fetus

Placenta, an organ that helps the baby grow using nutrients from its mother

Umbilical cord, a tube that connects the placenta to the fetus

Week 9

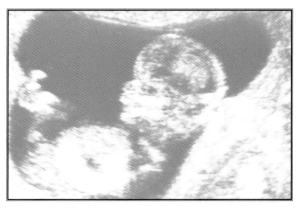

An ultrasound picture of a 12-week-old fetus

WATCHING BABIES GROW

In the 1950s, Scottish doctor Ian Donald developed a way to see a fetus inside the uterus, using a massive machine called an *ultrasound scanner*. The scanner bounces waves of sound off the fetus, and a computer draws a picture.

Sickness and health

The black death

In the 14th century, a deadly disease, known as the black death, or bubonic plague, ravaged Europe. No one knew what caused it or how it spread. Many people believed it was a punishment from God.

By the 20th century, scientists determined that the plague was spread by rats...

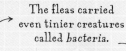

...that carried tiny fleas that jumped onto people and bit them.

The fleas carried even tinier creatures called *bacteria*.

German physician Robert Koch studied the disease tuberculosis in the 1880s. He proved that this, and many other diseases, are caused by micro-organisms called *bacteria*.

People bitten by the fleas were infected with the bacteria, and they fell ill with bubonic plague.

Infections

Sickness is usually caused by one of three types of infection: bacteria, a fungus or a virus.

This picture shows a chain of *streptococcus* bacteria at 8,000 times larger than actual size. This type of bacteria causes tonsillitis.

Here is a fungus called *trichophyton* magnified 3,000 times larger than actual size. It causes a skin disease known as athlete's foot.

Viruses are the smallest of all known micro-organisms. Here, you can see a flu virus surrounding a red blood cell, 7,000 times greater than actual size.

Fighting infections

Inside your blood there are cells known as *leukocytes*, that help your body fight infections. Here are some examples:

Dendritic cells identify things that don't belong in a person's body, such as bacteria and viruses.

Macrophages kill bacteria in your blood.

Natural Killer cells destroy other cells that have become diseased and may harm the body.

(All these leukocytes are shown 6,000 times greater than actual size.)

Some kinds of leukocytes literally eat bacteria and viruses, in a process called *phagocytosis*.

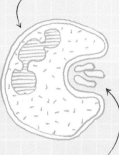

Macrophage

Bacteria

The macrophage gradually engulfs the bacteria...

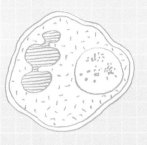

...then dissolves them.

DANGEROUS DOCTORS

For thousands of years, doctors all over the world believed the best way to heal a sick person was to drain 'bad blood'. But, in most cases, this made each patient suffer for longer, because blood is vital for healing.

ANTIGENS AND ANTIBODIES

Human bodies can detect the presence of viruses and bacteria because they contain unique parts called *antigens*. Leukocytes work together to find antigens and create new parts called *antibodies* that can trap and destroy antigens.

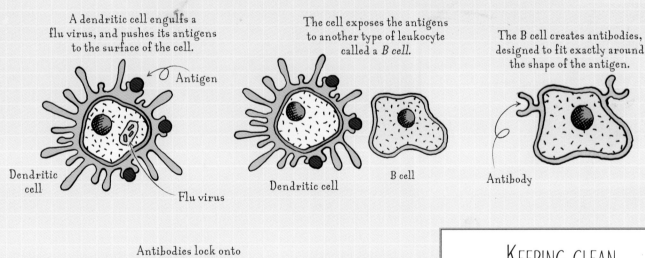

A dendritic cell engulfs a flu virus, and pushes its antigens to the surface of the cell.

Antigen

Dendritic cell

Flu virus

The cell exposes the antigens to another type of leukocyte called a *B cell*.

Dendritic cell

B cell

The B cell creates antibodies, designed to fit exactly around the shape of the antigen.

Antibody

Antibodies lock onto the antigens, and carry the trapped virus to an organ near the stomach called the *spleen*.

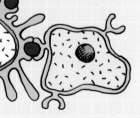

Antigens from the same virus always have the same shape.

Most antibodies only fit around one kind of antigen.

The spleen filters the viruses out of the bloodstream, and helps make new antibodies.

It usually takes a few days for antibodies to capture and filter out a whole infection.

KEEPING CLEAN

In 1847, Hungarian doctor Ignaz Semmelweis suggested that doctors and nurses should wash their hands before treating patients, to keep infections from spreading.

At first, people thought this was ridiculous. But by the time he died, in 1865, most doctors were following his advice.

DAMAGE AND REPAIR

Bodies can often repair themselves when they are damaged.
But sometimes they need help.

CUTS

Some injuries can tear a blood vessel, making you bleed. Very healthy people can survive even if they lose 40% of their blood.

This picture shows blood cells starting to flow out of a broken blood vessel. These blood cells are shown at 600 times actual size.

CLOTTING

Tiny cells in your blood called *platelets* stop bleeding by creating a mesh to trap blood cells.

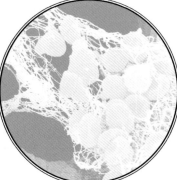

In this magnified photo, you can see platelets as tiny pink blobs inside the white mesh.

FRACTURES

When your bones get hit very hard, they can break. Any kind of crack in a bone is called a fracture.

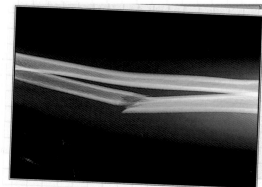

This X-ray shows a fractured radius – one of the bones in your arm.

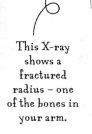

Bones can build new cells and repair fractures themselves.

Doctors often wrap the arm in a dressing, then cover it with a tough plaster cast. This keeps the bones still so they can heal cleanly.

CANCER

Sometimes cells in part of your body multiply and grow in ways they shouldn't. This is a sign of a dangerous disease called *cancer*.

Cancer cells

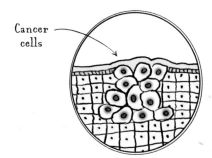

FIGHTING CANCER

There are two common ways to combat cancer: *chemotherapy* and *radiation therapy*, or *radiotherapy*.

Cells destroyed by radiation

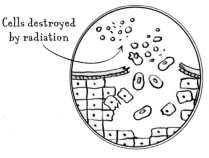

Radiotherapy works by bombarding the affected cells with beams of radiation. The beams are very precise, but they can destroy some healthy cells, too.

Chemotherapy means giving a patient drugs that stop cancerous cells from multiplying.

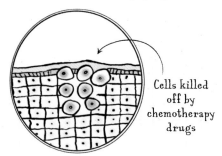

Cells killed off by chemotherapy drugs

Chemotherapy drugs often affect healthy cells, too. While taking the drugs, patients find their hair falls out, and they get sick easily, too.

SPARE PARTS

Sometimes, parts of the body can break down so badly that the best way to fix them is to replace them with a new part.

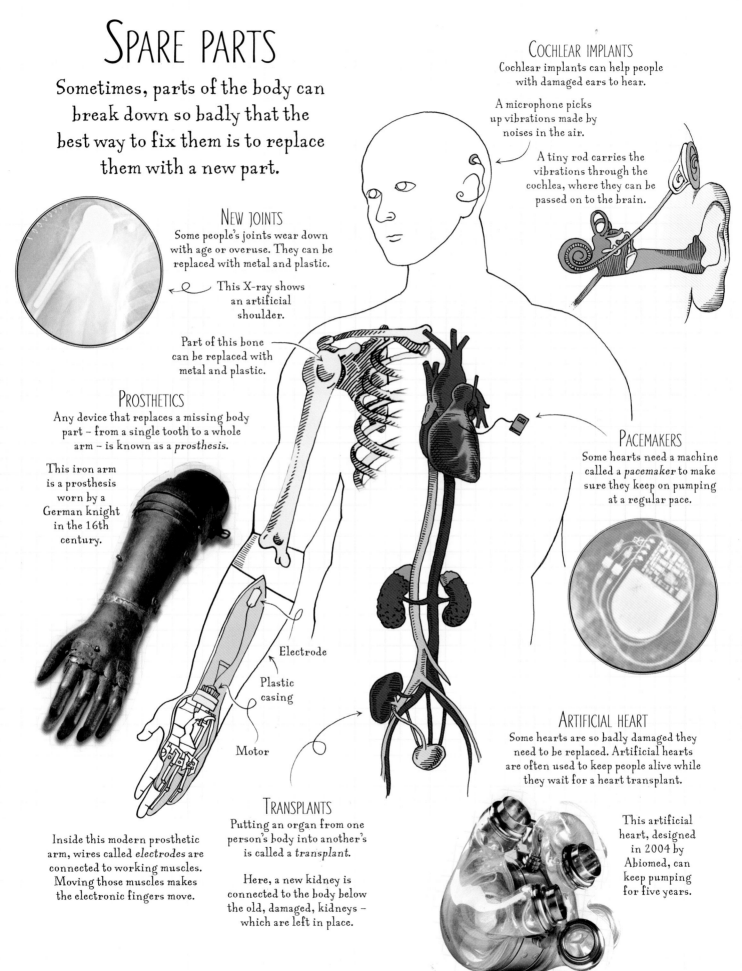

COCHLEAR IMPLANTS
Cochlear implants can help people with damaged ears to hear.

A microphone picks up vibrations made by noises in the air.

A tiny rod carries the vibrations through the cochlea, where they can be passed on to the brain.

NEW JOINTS
Some people's joints wear down with age or overuse. They can be replaced with metal and plastic.

This X-ray shows an artificial shoulder.

Part of this bone can be replaced with metal and plastic.

PROSTHETICS
Any device that replaces a missing body part – from a single tooth to a whole arm – is known as a *prosthesis*.

This iron arm is a prosthesis worn by a German knight in the 16th century.

Electrode

Plastic casing

Motor

Inside this modern prosthetic arm, wires called *electrodes* are connected to working muscles. Moving those muscles makes the electronic fingers move.

PACEMAKERS
Some hearts need a machine called a *pacemaker* to make sure they keep on pumping at a regular pace.

TRANSPLANTS
Putting an organ from one person's body into another's is called a *transplant*.

Here, a new kidney is connected to the body below the old, damaged, kidneys – which are left in place.

ARTIFICIAL HEART
Some hearts are so badly damaged they need to be replaced. Artificial hearts are often used to keep people alive while they wait for a heart transplant.

This artificial heart, designed in 2004 by Abiomed, can keep pumping for five years.

Facts and records

Every single person is unique – but all human bodies need the same things to survive. Unique combinations of DNA, lifestyle and force of will mean that human beings set new records for body shape, size and achievement all the time.

Tallest

The tallest person in recorded history was an American man named Robert Wadlow. He was 2.72m (8ft, 11in) when he died in 1940.

Shortest

The smallest person in recorded history is still alive. He is Chandra Bahadur Dangi from Nepal, who stands just 54.60cm (1ft, 9in) tall.

Fastest

The fastest running race in the world is the 100m sprint.

The current world record holder is Jamaican Usain Bolt. In 2009, he ran 100m in 9.58 seconds, reaching a top speed of around 45km/h (28mph).

Long, longer, longest

Some parts of the body, such as hair and fingernails, just keep on growing. It doesn't hurt to cut hair and nails because the cells on the ends are dead.

George Gabler's whiskers stretched 71cm (28in) across. When it was measured in the 19th century, this was a world record. The current record, held by Ram Singh Chauhan of India, is a vast 429cm (14ft).

Memory test

The human brain has a huge capacity to store information, although it is hard to test the limits.

In 2005, Chinese student Lu Chao recited the number known as 'pi' to 67,890 digits, all from memory – a record achievement.

Oldest

The oldest person in recorded history was Frenchwoman Jeanne Calment, who died in 1997 at the age of 122 years and 164 days.

Most children

18th-century Russian couple Mr. and Mrs. Feodor Vassilyev had 69 children together. This total included four sets of quadruplets and seven sets of triplets.

Strangest diet

French entertainer Michel Lotito found fame by eating a variety of machines, including bicycles, TV sets and even an entire plane.

Lotito broke metal parts into pieces, and swallowed them with oil and water. He died of natural causes in 2007, at age 57.

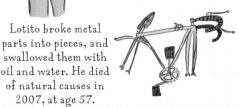

LEFT TO RIGHT

A very small number of people are born with their internal organs positioned the opposite way.

This is known as *situs inversus*. Most people born this way live out healthy lives.

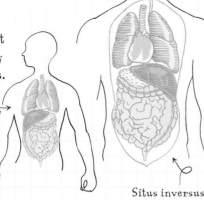

How organs are usually arranged

Situs inversus organs

IDENTIFYING MARKS

Everyone, including identical twins, has a unique pattern of tiny grooves on their fingertips. The grooves help with gripping things.

Detectives often look for fingerprints at crime scenes. If they can match a fingerprint to a suspect's fingers, it can help prove that person committed the crime.

TOO HOT

Bodies are designed to stay at around 37°C (98.6°F). It can be fatal for a body to get hotter than 40°C (104°F) for too long.

TOO COLD

Bodies that falls below 30°C (68°F) start to shut down. Prolonged exposure to cold is often fatal.

In 1912, the extreme cold of Antarctica killed a five-man team of British explorers. They successfully reached the South Pole, but died on the way back.

SURVIVAL CHECKLIST

Every human body needs a constant supply of food, water, air and sleep to survive.

- **Every hour** — Without a steady supply of oxygen, you would die in under an hour.

- **Every day** — Human bodies are designed to sleep for at least a few hours every day. The record for staying awake is under three weeks.

- **Every week** — Without water, you would die in less than a week.

- **Every month** — Without food, you would die within four to eight weeks.

TOO DEEP

Really deep underwater, the pressure can crush a person's organs – a painful, and often fatal, condition known as *barotrauma*.

The toughest diving suits, such as the Newtsuit shown here, allow wearers to descend over 600m (2,000ft) deep.

The recommended limit for divers without a suit is only 100m (330ft).

THE HISTORY OF MEDICINE

For thousands of years, doctors, physicians and surgeons have found new ways to heal people. This timeline shows some of the great milestones.

Around 5,000 years ago

Legendary Chinese ruler Shennong tested hundreds of herbal remedies and wrote a book describing their effects.

Around 4,000 years ago

The earliest recorded prosthetic limb, an iron leg, was fitted to Indian woman warrior Vishpala.

This prosthetic toe was made by Egyptians around 2,500 years ago.

Around 2,500 years ago

Greek doctor Hippocrates began the tradition of swearing never to harm a patient. Doctors today still make this promise, known as 'the Hippocratic Oath'.

Around 2,000 years ago

Greek scholar Galen wrote a book on anatomy. Zhang Zhongjing wrote a handbook of medicine in China. Both books were studied by doctors for the next thousand years.

Around 1,000 years ago

Persian scholar Ibn Sina explained how to test medicines properly to prove they work.

17th century

Scientists Robert Hooke and Antonie van Leeuwenhoek built powerful microscopes and discovered cells and bacteria.

1740s

Scottish doctor James Lind discovered that eating citrus fruits prevents a disease called scurvy. The active ingredient is later named vitamin C.

1790s

English doctor Edward Jenner invented a new treatment called a vaccine. His vaccine stopped people from catching smallpox, a deadly disease.

1840s

U.S. dentist William Morton developed an inhaler filled with ether gas. The gas made patients sleep during surgery, and numbed their senses so they didn't feel drilling or pulling.

1850s

British nurse Florence Nightingale proved that more soldiers died from bad conditions in hospitals than died from wounds in battle.

Nightingale drew a chart comparing causes of death:

⬤ Death from wounds
⬤ Death from hospital infection
⬤ Any other cause

1880s

German physician Robert Koch proved that many diseases are spread by bacteria. He identified the bacteria that cause tuberculosis and cholera.

1895

German physicist Wilhelm Röntgen discovered that X-rays can shine through skin to show bones and organs.

1901

Austrian doctor Karl Landsteiner discovered that blood exists in several different types.

People with matching types can give each other blood, a procedure called transfusion.

1923

Scottish biologist Alexander Fleming discovered a fungus called *penicillium* that kills bacteria.

1930s

The first electron microscopes are built. Doctors can see viruses in action for the first time.

A smallpox virus magnified to 28,500 times actual size

1945

A team of scientists discovered the chemical structure of *penicillium*. They made a drug from it, called *penicillin*, that cures all kinds of infections.

British chemist Dorothy Hodgkin built this model of the chemicals that make *penicillium*.

1947

U.S. doctor Stephen Hudack successfully implanted an artificial hip joint, to replace worn out hip bones.

X-ray showing an artificial hip

1952

U.S. doctors Alfred Hershey and Martha Chase proved that DNA contains a chemical code for building bodies.

1978

A baby girl is born using a new technique known as IVF, or *in vitro fertilization*. Her parents' sperm and egg were fused in a glass dish, then implanted into the mother's uterus.

To make IVF more precise, doctors can use a procedure called intracytoplasmic sperm injection. An individual sperm is injected directly into the cytoplasm of an egg.

The egg is braced against a pipette to keep it still.

1990

Doctors begin to experiment with *gene therapy*, a method of curing people who suffer from inherited conditions.

21st century

Ghanaian-American engineer Kwabena Boahen is developing a bionic eye to replace damaged eyes.

GLOSSARY

This page explains some of the words used in the book, and describes what different parts of the body do. Words written in *italic* type have an entry of their own.

An adult's heart is about the size of a fist.

The brain is one of the few parts of the body that doesn't feel pain.

ANTIBODIES Parts made by certain *leukocytes* that can find and destroy *antigens*.

ANTIGENS Unique parts found in *viruses* and *bacteria*.

BACTERIA Tiny creatures that live inside bodies. Some can attack *cells* and make a person sick.

BONE MARROW *Tissue* on the inside of some bones, where red blood cells are made.

BRAIN The main *organ* in the head that controls the body and creates conscious thought.

CARBON DIOXIDE A waste gas, produced by the body when it uses *oxygen* to do work.

CARTILAGE A material like bone, but softer and more flexible.

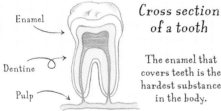

Enamel

Dentine

Pulp

Cross section of a tooth

The enamel that covers teeth is the hardest substance in the body.

CELL A tiny living unit. Each part of the body is made of billions of cells.

CHROMOSOME One of 46 tiny blobs found in the nucleus of most *cells*, made of *DNA*.

CIRCULATION The movement of blood and *oxygen* around the body.

CLOTTING The way blood thickens to block up a cut.

COCHLEA A spiral-shaped chamber inside each ear that helps convert vibrations into sounds.

COLON The large *intestine*.

DIAPHRAGM A muscle in the middle of body that helps expand and contract the lungs.

DIGESTION The action of breaking down food and absorbing nutrients from it.

DNA A complex chemical made up of millions of *genes*.

EMBRYO One of the first stages of life, when a body is made of a handful of *cells*.

EPIGLOTTIS A small flap that stops food from going down the throat.

FETUS A baby still inside its mother's *uterus*.

FUNGUS A living thing that can grow on or inside parts of the body.

GAMETE A *cell* that contains only 23 *chromosomes* in its nucleus. Two gametes fuse to create a new life.

GENE A small section of *DNA* that carries information telling *cells* what to do.

GLAND A small *organ*, or part of an organ, that makes and releases *hormones*.

HEART An *organ* in the chest that pumps blood around the body.

HORMONE A chemical that gives instructions to *organs*.

INFECTION A disease caused by a micro-organism, such as *bacteria* or a *fungus*.

INSULIN A *hormone* that regulates the amount of sugar in the body.

INTESTINES A long set of tubes that connects the stomach to the rectum. They absorb nutrients and water from food.

KIDNEYS A pair of *organs* in the lower back that keeps water in the body clean.

LEUKOCYTES *Cells* in the blood that fight *infections*.

LIGAMENT A stringy *tissue* that connects bones together.

LIVER A major *organ* that helps break down food, filter blood, and remove poisons.

LYMPH A liquid that helps keep bodies healthy.

LYMPHATIC SYSTEM A network of tubes that runs in between *organs* and blood vessels, containing a liquid called *lymph*.

The body has two kidneys, but only needs one to survive.

LUNGS Major *organs* in the chest that absorb and expel gases, especially *oxygen* and *carbon dioxide*.

NERVOUS SYSTEM A network of *cells*, connected to the *brain*, that sends messages all over the body.

NEURONS Nerve cells in the *brain*.

ORGAN A body part such as the eyes, lungs, skin or brain, that does a particular job.

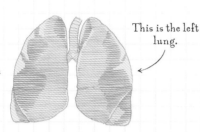

The left lung has a slightly smaller capacity than the right, to make room for the heart.

This is the left lung.

OVARIES *Organs* found only in women that make and store eggs.

OXYGEN A gas the body needs so that *cells*, *organs* and muscles can work.

PANCREAS An *organ* that releases *hormones* and *digestive* juices.

PREGNANT When a woman has a *fetus* inside her, she is pregnant.

PROSTHESIS An artificial object used to replace a missing body part.

SEM Scanning Electron Microscope, a machine used to look at really tiny things, such as *cells*, *bacteria* and *viruses*.

The spleen, shown here, helps bodies stay healthy. Human bodies can survive if the spleen is removed, but they will get sick more easily.

SPLEEN An *organ* found behind the stomach that helps keep blood clean and healthy.

STOMACH An *organ* that helps break down food and absorb nutrients.

TENDON A *tissue* that connects muscles to bones.

TESTES A pair of *organs* found only in men that make and store sperm, the male *gamete*.

TISSUE A group of *cells* that look and act the same, such as muscle tissue.

TRANSPLANT An *organ* or *tissue* donated by one person to another to do the work of a diseased or damaged organ.

ULTRASOUND A kind of camera that uses sound waves to see inside the body.

URINE A liquid made by the *kidneys* that contains water and toxins filtered out of the body.

UTERUS An *organ* found only in woman that can support a growing *fetus*.

VIRUS A micro-organism, often smaller than a *cell*, that can attack and damage cells.

X-RAY A kind of photograph, made using beams called X-rays, that can show the inside of a living body.

LATIN AND GREEK

Doctors often describe parts of the body using their names in Latin or Ancient Greek. Here are some common examples:

- ● CARDIAC To do with the heart
- ◐ PULMONARY To do with the lungs
- ○ HEPATIC To do with the liver
- ○ CRANIAL To do with the head
- ○ OSTEO To do with the bones
- ◔ BRACHIAL To do with the arm
- ◑ NEURAL To do with the brain
- ◔ GASTRIC To do with the stomach

Acknowledgments

Every effort has been made to trace and acknowledge ownership of copyright. If any rights have been omitted, the publishers offer to rectify this in any future editions following notification. The publishers are grateful to the following individuals and organizations for their permission to reproduce material on the following pages:

Cover X-ray of a head: © Phototake inc. / Alamy; SEM of spongy bone: © Paul Gunning / Science Photo Library; SEM of an embryo: © Dr. Yorgos Nikas / Science Photo Library

p4-5 Skeleton and bones X-ray of a hand: © Science Photo Library

p6-7 Muscle power Skeletal muscle: © Dr. Gladden Willis / Visuals Unlimited, Inc. / Science Photo Library

p8-9 Circulation Red blood cells: © Susumu Nishinaga / Science Photo Library

p12-13 Brain power Phrenology map: © Classic Image / Alamy; MRI scan: © Sovereign, Ism / Science Photo Library

p14-15 Sensing the world Surface of the tongue: © CNRI / Science Photo Library

p16-17 Looking closer Cheek cells: both © Dr. Gopal Murti / Science Photo Library; Animalcules: © Pictorial Press Ltd / Alamy

p18-19 The secret in the cells Chromosomes: © Power And Syred / Science Photo Library

p20-21 Making new bodies Egg cell: © Andy Walker, Midland Fertility Services / Science Photo Library; Sperm cell: © Dr. Richard Kessel & Dr. Gene Shih, Visuals Unlimited / Science Photo Library; Ultrasound scan: © Gustoimages / Science Photo Library

p22-23 Sickness and health Streptococcus bacteria: © Pasieka / Science Photo Library; Trichophyton fungus: © Biophoto Associates / Science Photo Library; Flu virus: © Nibsc / Science Photo Library; Macrophage: © Steve Gschmeissner / Science Photo Library; Natural Killer cell: © Eye Of Science / Science Photo Library; Dendritic blood cell: © Dr. Olivier Schwartz, Institute Pasteur / Science Photo Library

p24-25 Damage and repair Bleeding: © Photo Insolite Realite / Science Photo Library; Clotting: © Susumu Nishinaga / Science Photo Library; Fractured radius: © Sovereign / Ism / Science Photo Library; Artificial shoulder: © Kallista Images / Visuals Unlimited / Corbis; Iron hand: © Science Museum / Science & Society Picture Library; Pacemaker: © Apogee / Science Photo Library; Artificial heart: courtesy of Abiomed

p26-27 Facts and records Usain Bolt: © Aflo Foto Agency / Alamy; Longest moustache: © Bettmann / CORBIS; Scott's expedition: © Ria Novosti / Science Photo Library; Newtsuit: © Alexis Rosenfeld / Science Photo Library

p28-29 The history of medicine Prosthetic toe: © AFP / Getty Images; Smallpox bacteria: © Eye Of Science / Science Photo Library; model of penicillium: © Science Museum, London; X-ray of artificial hip: © Miriam Maslo / Science Photo Library; Intracytoplasmic sperm injection: © Hank Morgan / Science Photo Library

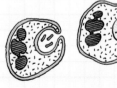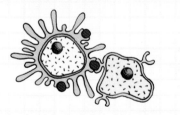

Edited by Jane Chisholm

Additional design by Samantha Barrett and Tom Lalonde

Usborne Internet Links

For links to websites where you can find out more about the human body, go to the Usborne Quicklinks website at **www.usborne.com/quicklinks** and type in the keywords '**Human body sticker book**'. Please read our internet safety guidelines on the Usborne Quicklinks website. Usborne Publishing is not responsible and does not accept liability for the availability or content of any website other than its own, or for any exposure to harmful, offensive, or inaccurate material which may appear on the Web or any damage or loss caused by viruses that may be downloaded as a result of browsing the sites it recommends.

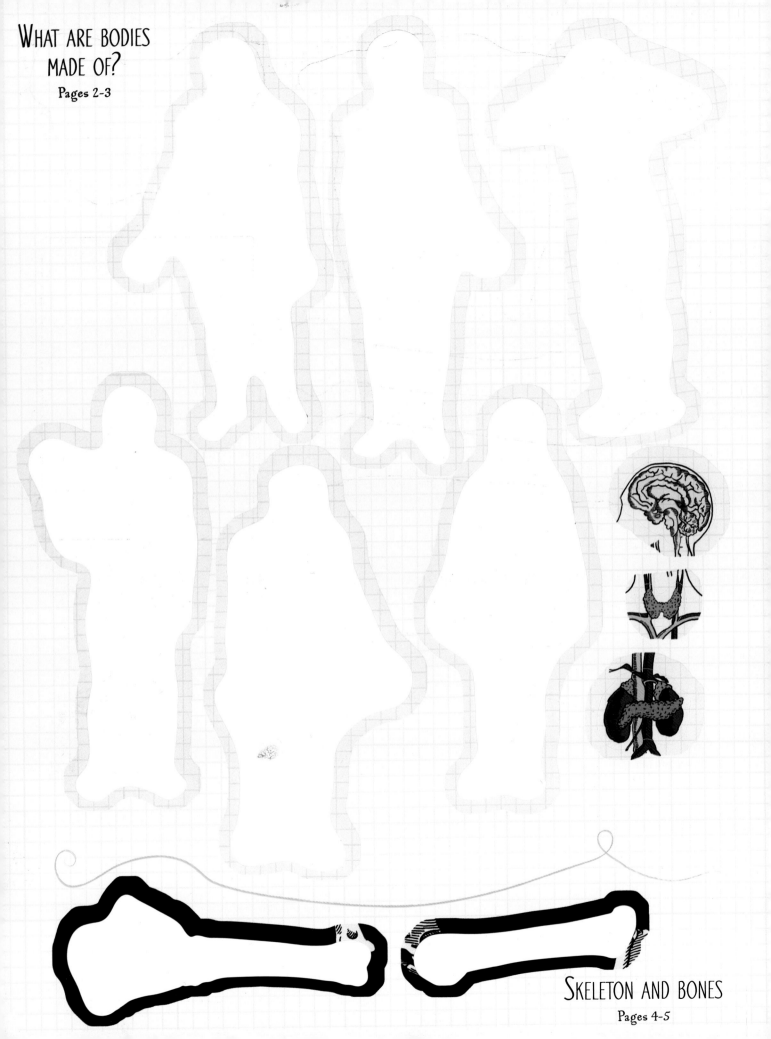

SKELETON AND BONES

Pages 4-5

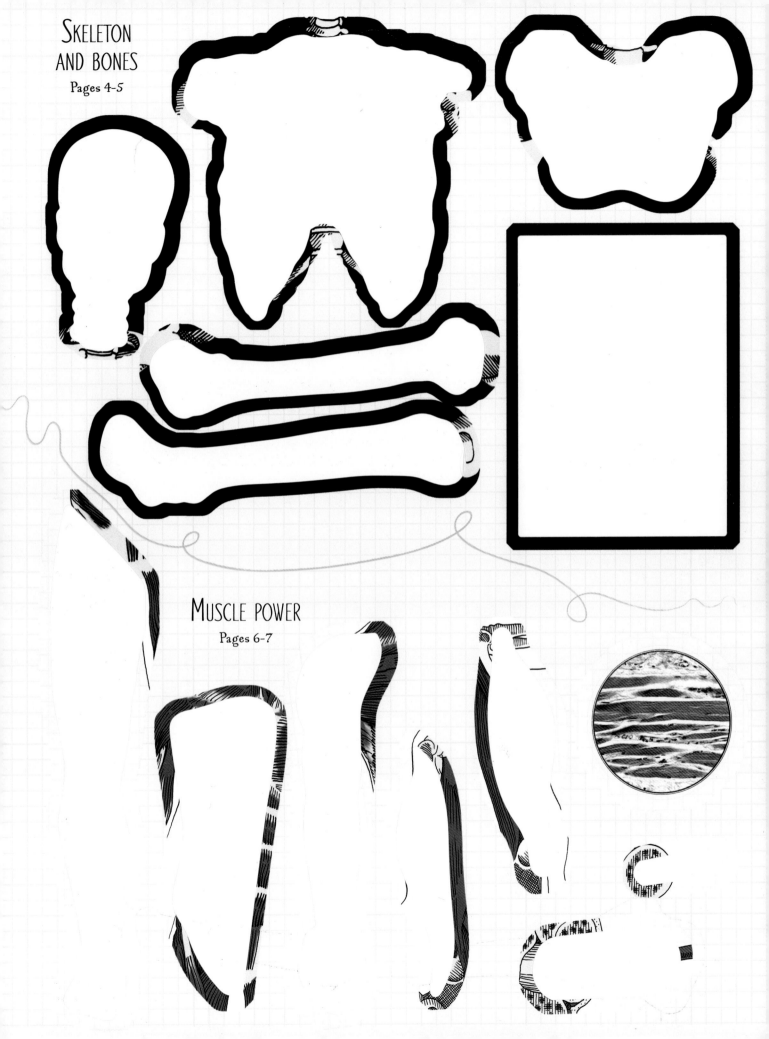

SKELETON AND BONES
Pages 4-5

MUSCLE POWER
Pages 6-7

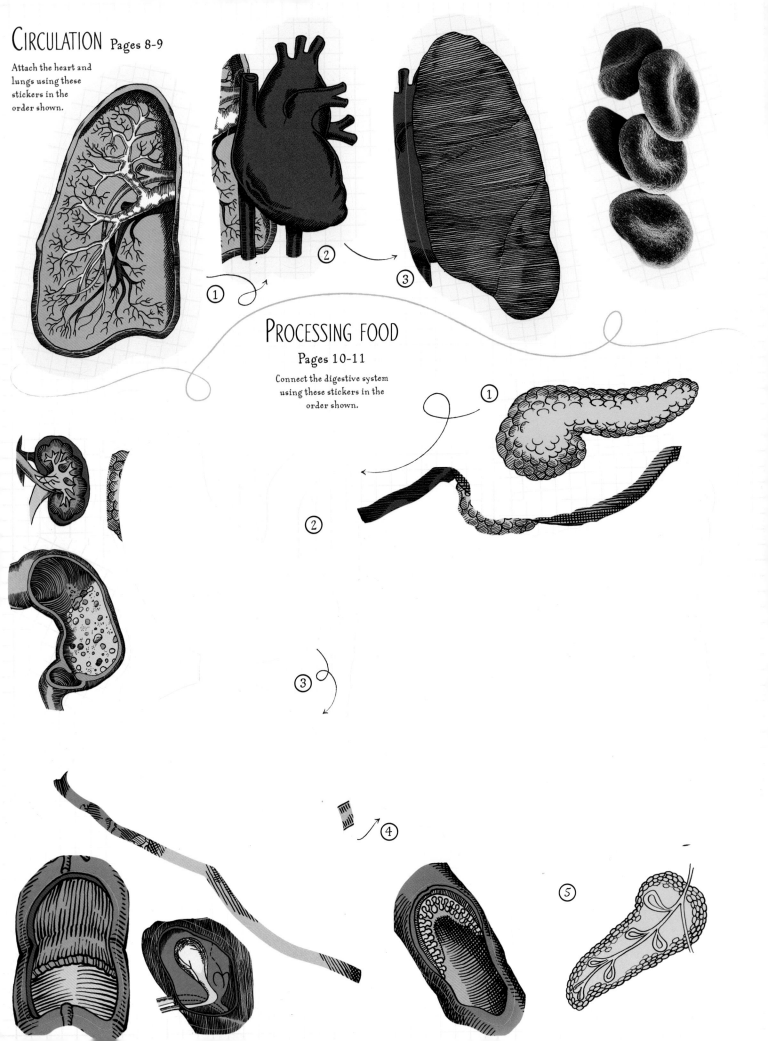

CIRCULATION Pages 8-9

Attach the heart and lungs using these stickers in the order shown.

① ② ③

PROCESSING FOOD

Pages 10-11

Connect the digestive system using these stickers in the order shown.

① ② ③ ④ ⑤

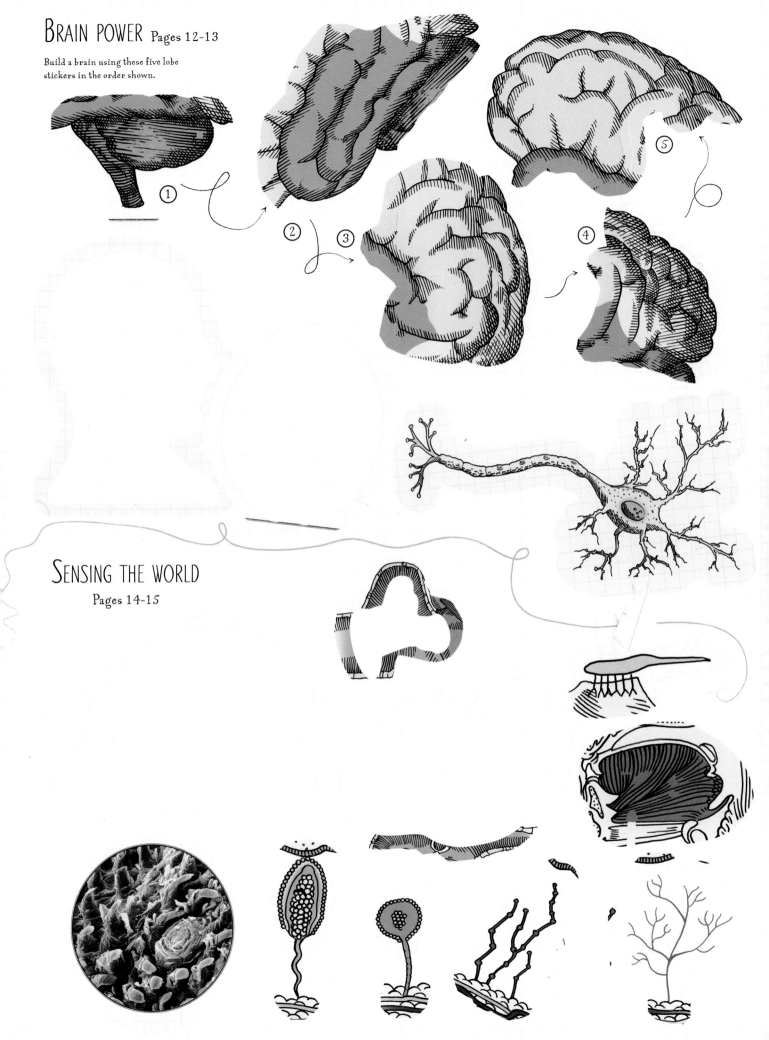

Brain power Pages 12-13

Build a brain using these five lobe stickers in the order shown.

① ② ③ ④ ⑤

Sensing the world

Pages 14-15

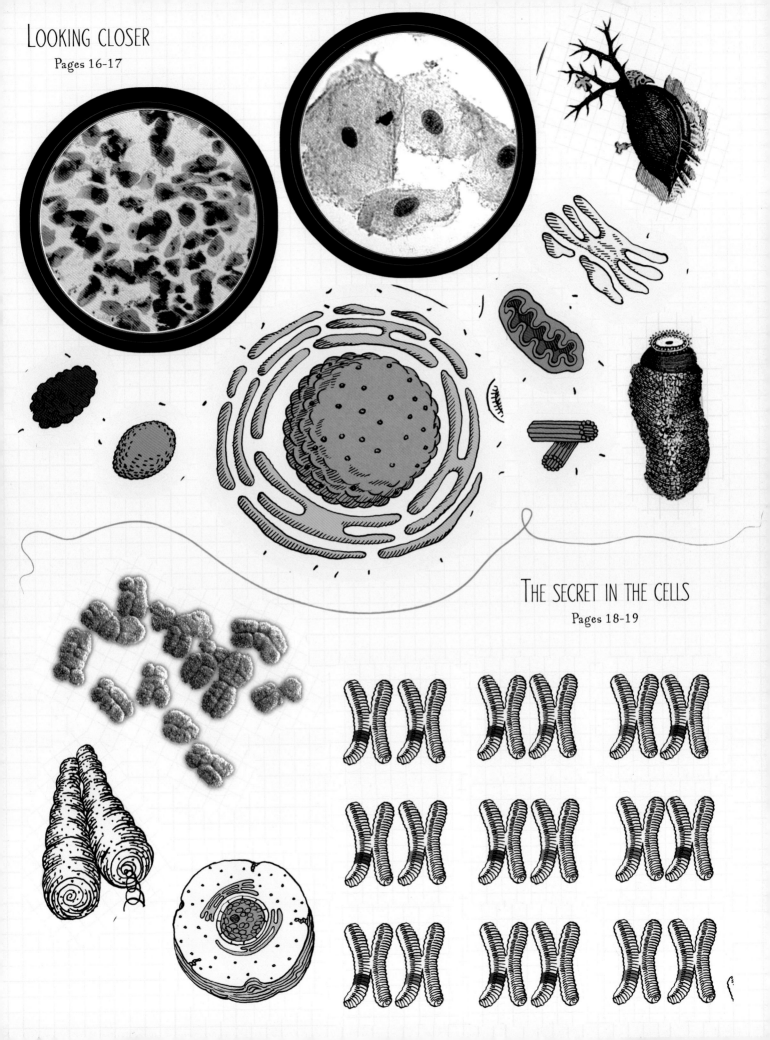

The secret in the cells
Pages 18–19

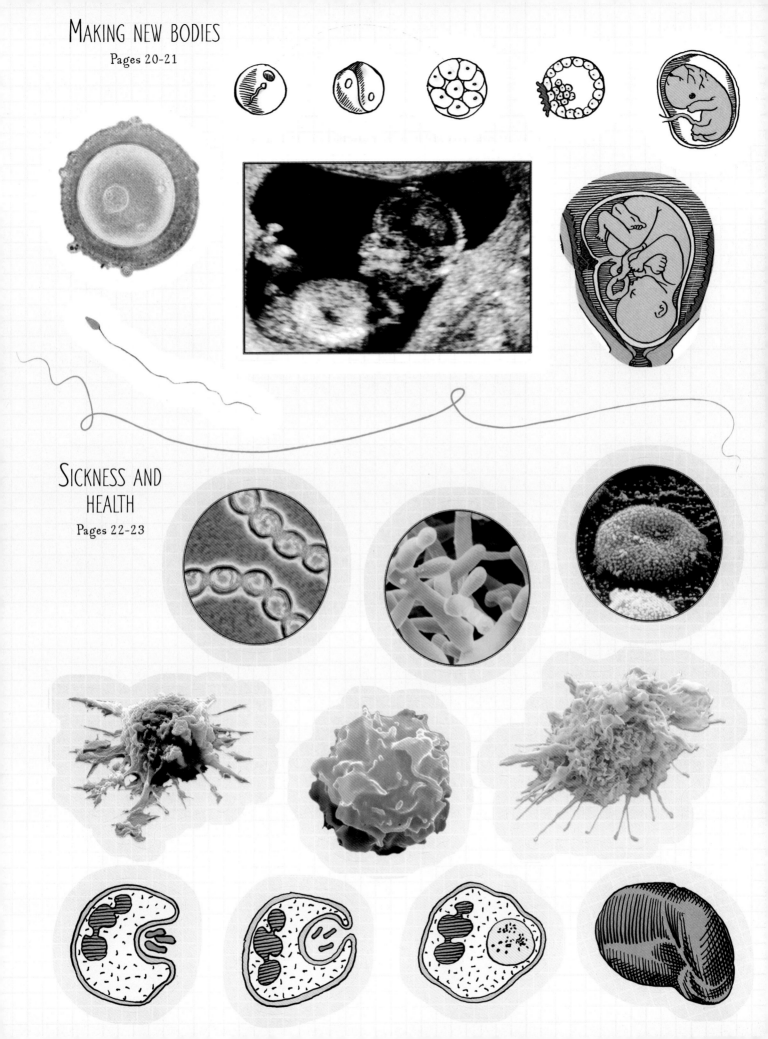

Making new bodies
Pages 20-21

Sickness and health
Pages 22-23

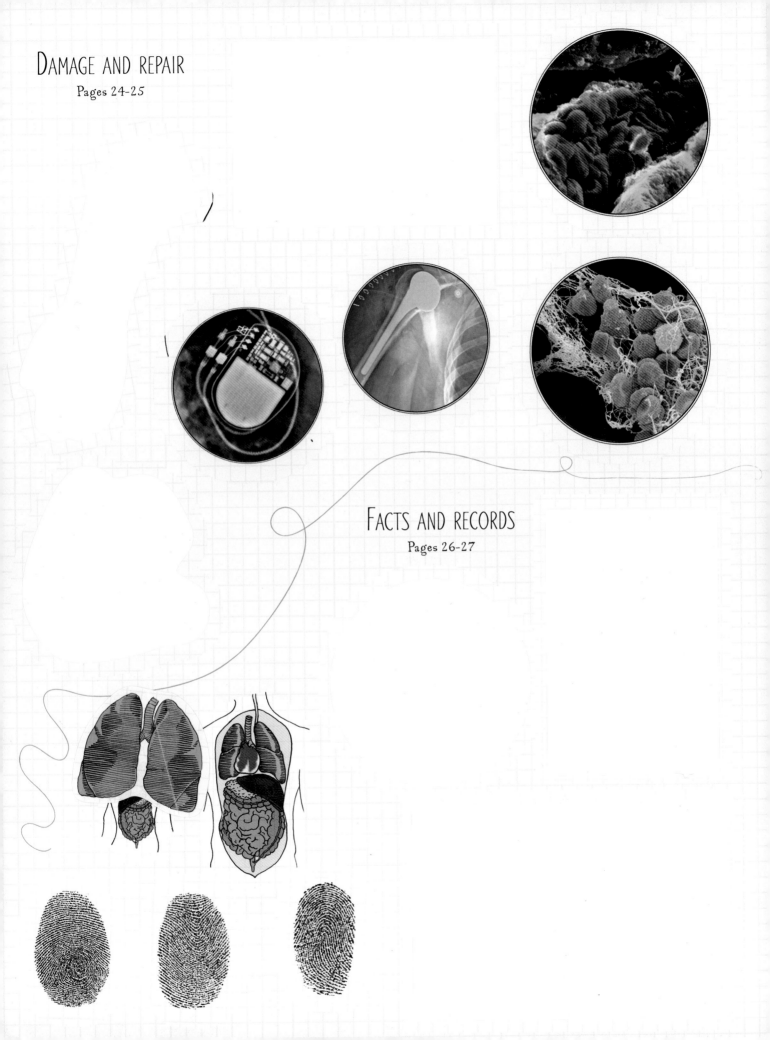

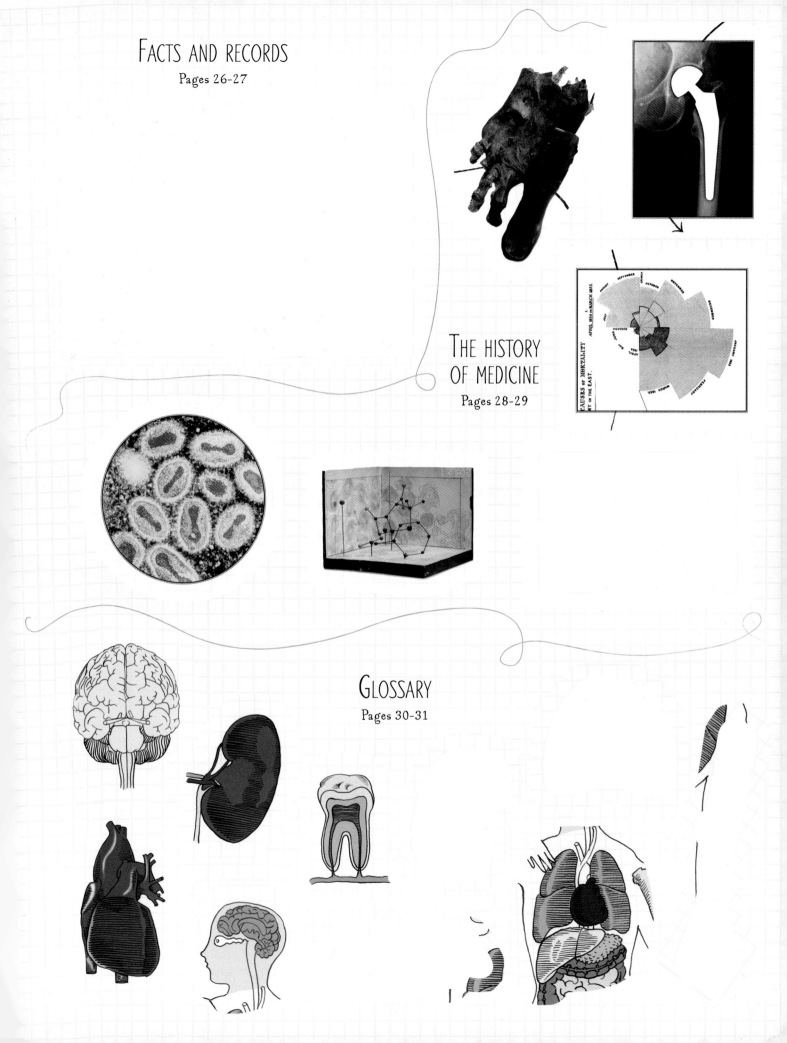